# Let's Live....

# ALOHA

Gerry Ebalaroza-Tunnell, Ph.D.

Illustrated by Qoni Fadhilah

© 2024

*This book is dedicated to my grandchildren,*
*Lyric, Kai'mana, and Kapi'olani*

**Aloha**, friends!

My name is **Dr. G** and I'd like to teach you about my favorite word, **Aloha**. **Aloha** is a powerful word that comes from the islands of Hawaii and has many beautiful meanings.

Aloha can mean hello, goodbye, and even love!
Aloha is a word that teaches us <u>how</u> to **live**.

Living **Aloha** creates kindness, peace, and love in our homes, schools, towns, and cities by creating these ways of being within ourselves!

Living **Aloha** means that we are kind to our friends
and think about their feelings.
Just as we would like them to do for us!

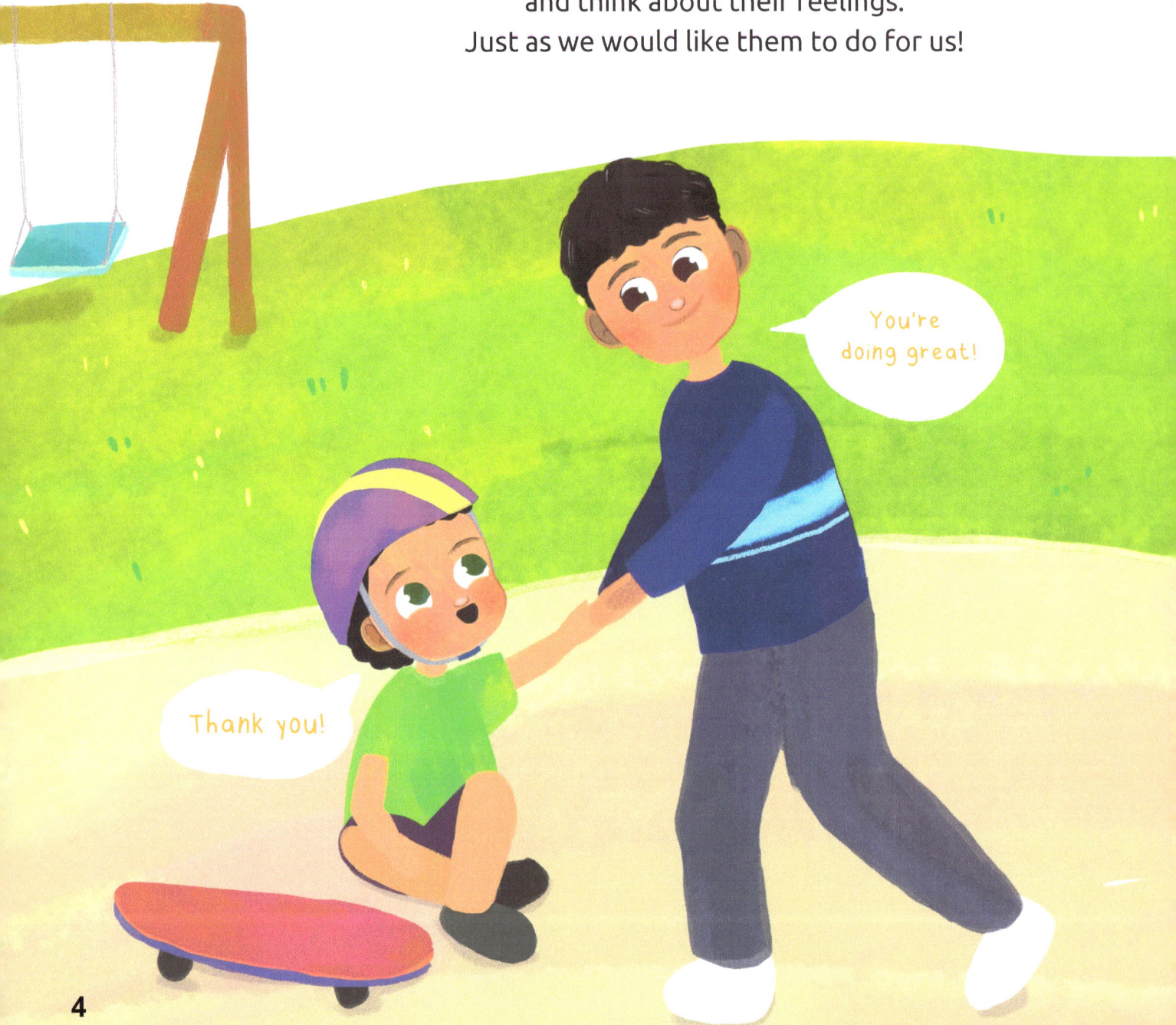

You're
doing great!

Thank you!

We say kind words to friends, like *Good Job* and *Thank You*, to show our care and appreciation for them.

When we do this, it makes us happy and makes our friends happy too!

ALO

I made up a fun game to help me remember how to be friendly, make new friends, and live **Aloha** everyday!

6    Would you like to learn my game of **A.L.O.H.A.** so you can live **Aloha** too?

It starts with **A**...

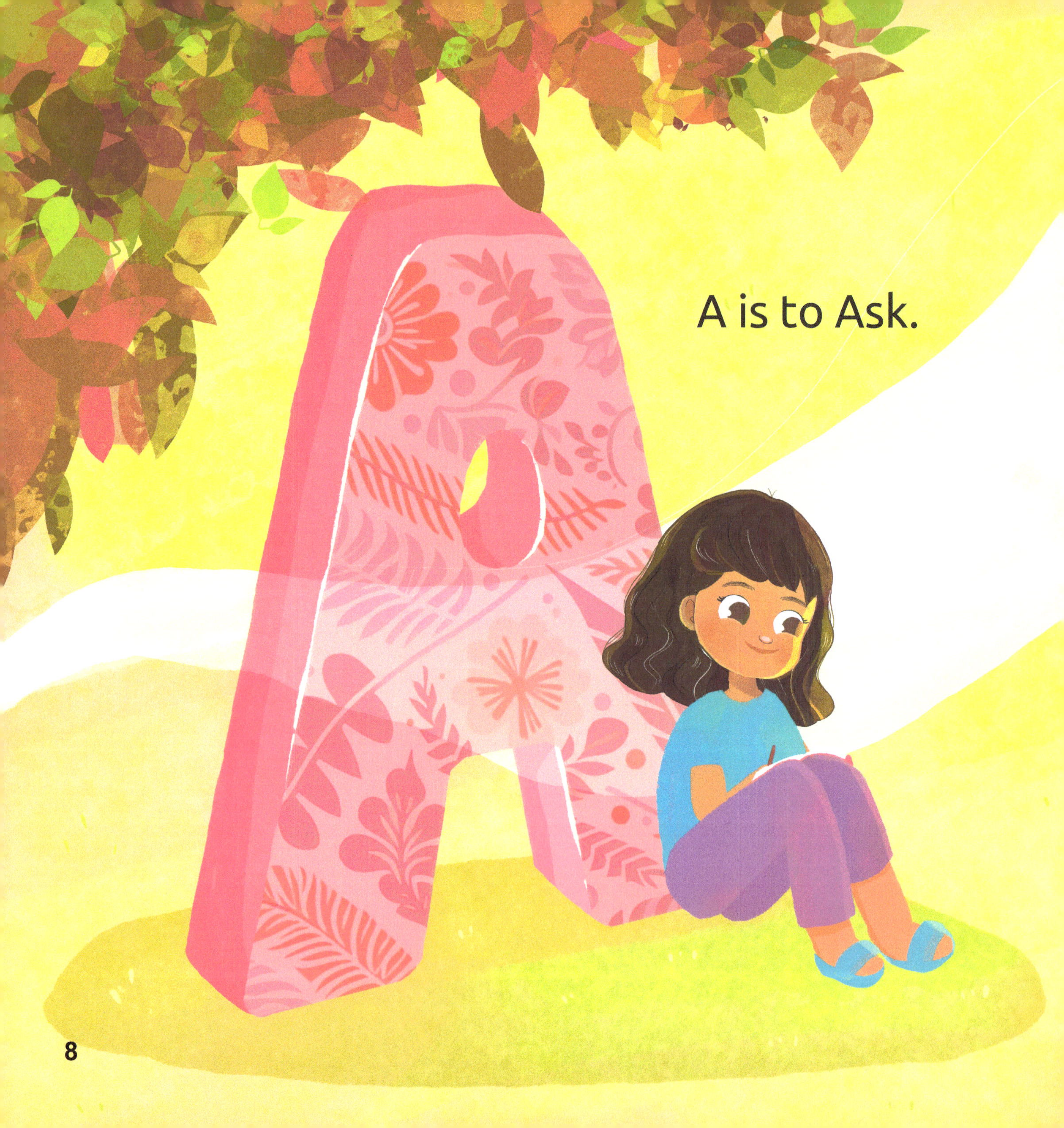

A is to Ask.

When you are curious about something,
like a new friend or a different way of doing things,
it's good to **Ask** questions. This way, you can learn more
and find out all kinds of interesting things!

Journal

.Today I learned about
the power of asking
good questions.

Can you think of a fun or interesting question
to **ASK** someone today?

# L is to Listen.

**Listening** is just as powerful as **Asking**! When you learn to **Listen**, you hear other people's stories, ideas, and the lessons they have to teach you.

We show that we care when we **Listen** to others by helping them feel heard, just like you are listening to my story right now!

That makes me feel good! Thanks, Friends!

my favorite things

Library Show & tell

O is to Observe.

**Observing** is like being a super scientist!
You can **observe** how your tummy flip-flops when you're nervous.
You can **observe** how your **heart** beats faster when you're excited - it's your body's way of telling you how it's feeling.

All you have to do is **Observe**!

I'll show you how.

Take three deep breaths and **Ask** silently, to yourself,

How am I feeling right now?

Now, **Listen** for the answer by **Observing** what your body is telling you.

How does your body feel?

# H is for **Heart**.

The **Heart** is where all your *kindness*, *peace* and *love* reside. When you share these feelings, you give others the superpowers of your **Heart**!

I will show you a very special way to activate your **Heart** superpower ...

Place your hand over your **Heart.**

With your hands on your **Heart**, think of something you are thankful for,

like someone who loves you, or warm cookies,

or the giggles of your best friend when you make silly faces!

Silently... think to yourself,

I am thankful for _____.

Have you got it?

Hold that feeling and imagine it filling your heart like a balloon full of sunshine.

Hold your gratitude as we take three long, deep breaths together:

In through your nose.

Out through your mouth.

Ready? Here we go...

**19**

IN 1 . . .

2 . . .

3 . . .

20

OUT 1...

2...

3...

IN 1... 2... 3... OUT

1...  2...  3...

23

IN 1...

2...

3...

OUT 1 . . . 2 . . . 3 . . .

How does your heart feel?

# A is for Adapt.

**Adapt** means to make a change in your behavior, attitude, or how you think of others. It's how you grow on the inside!

When you **Ask** good questions, truly **Listen** to yourself and others, **Observe** how your body responds, and stay in your **Heart**, you're ready to **Adapt** to new things.

How has my story of **Aloha** influenced your ability to **Adapt** in some way?

# Ask • Listen • Observe • Heart • Adapt

Every day is a chance to share your A.L.O.H.A with others!

Every kind word, caring act, and understanding of someone's feelings spreads the power of living **Aloha**.

Do you want to live **Aloha** with me?

*Then, let's all say it together!*

# Author Bio

Dr. Gerry Ebalaroza-Tunnell, affectionately known as Dr. G, is not only a beacon of the Aloha spirit but also a remarkable advocate for the principles of connection, compassion, and mutual prosperity. As the esteemed Founder and CEO of Co3: Co-Creating Cohesive Communities, she is dedicated to fostering transformative leadership and instigating systemic change that paves the way for cohesive communities to thrive.

Born and raised in the heart of Honolulu, Hawaii, Dr. G's roots run deep, allowing her to draw upon her ancestors' profound wisdom and cultural heritage. Her unwavering commitment to creating a better world is evident in every endeavor she undertakes. Dr. G's remarkable journey and relentless pursuit of positive change make her an inspiring figure, leaving an indelible mark on the lives of those fortunate enough to cross paths with her. She is the author of The Evolution of AloHā: Awakening the Breath of Life.

Dr. Gerry Ebalaroza-Tunnell
Author • Founder • Consultant
Co3 Consulting, LLC

www.ingramcontent.com/pod-product-compliance
Lightning Source LLC
Chambersburg PA
CBHW041539260326
41914CB00015B/1506